PORTSMOUTH
THEN & NOW

JOHN SADDEN &

MARK WINGHAM

The
History
Press

First published 2010

The History Press
The Mill, Brimscombe Port
Stroud, Gloucestershire, GL5 2QG
www.thehistorypress.co.uk

British Library Cataloguing in Publication Data.
A catalogue record for this book is available from the British Library.

ISBN 978 0 7524 5658 4

Typesetting and origination by The History Press
Printed in Malta
Manufacturing managed by Jellyfish Print Solutions Ltd

CONTENTS

HIGHLAND ROAD, EASTNEY, *c.* 1905. The Barrack Cellars (seen here behind the tram) was demolished in 1972 as a result of road widening to cope with the post-war increase in car ownership. Eastney Depot was opened in 1932, just around the corner on the left, and four years later the last tram ran between the Guildhall and Eastney, bringing the tramway era in the city to an end, to be replaced by that of the trolleybus (*see* page 31).

ACKNOWLEDGEMENTS

Thanks are due to Alan King and the staff of Portsmouth Central Library, who continue to provide an excellent service in the face of brutal Council cuts in opening hours and resources. Thanks also to Stella Jamieson (Verger) and Revd Canon Bob White for permitting access to St Mary's Church tower; Peter Rogers; Tim Runnacles; the late William Burbage; to John Anthony Portsmouth Football Club Westwood; to Portsmouth Grammar School Local History Club members Ethan Creamer, Jack Ross and David Simmonds for assisting with taking photographs in the High Street; and to Karen Sadden and Mrs M.C. Sadden; and to long-suffering postcard 'widow' Sally-Anne Wingham.

A CENTURY BEFORE television, computer games and Facebook monopolised children's spare time, before whittling gave way to Twittering, go-carts and handcarts fashioned from crates and perambulator wheels were popular and gave children and their fathers the opportunity to spend time together making the best cart in the street, in this case Wheatstone Road (*see* page 49), *c.* 1905.

INTRODUCTION

It was the world of our parents and our parents' parents – and yet it might have been a different planet. Roads devoid of cars, but with the occasional tram forcing a cyclist or the tradesman pulling his cart to take evasive action. Such was the pace of society – and transport – that walking between the tramlines offered little threat to life and limb, as you can see in Saxe Weimar (now Waverley) Road (page 57) or in Kingston Road (page 69). And if you get fed up waiting for the tram, why not just hop on a horse, like the rider in King's Road (page 76)?

There are family shops down nearly every street. Just look at the activity in Eastney Road (page 73). And how about the butcher's store in Albert Road (page 79)? Health and safety would be swarming over the meat hanging outside the premises if such a picture was taken today.

Uniformed soldiers and sailors were almost part of the furniture on 'civvy street' in Pompey before the First World War. The Royal Marine in Highland Road (page 25) looks like he's getting in some practise for the parade ground as he smartly puts his best foot forward, perhaps heading back to Eastney Barracks, while sailors are enjoying window shopping in Russell Street (page 87).

You can almost spot a policeman on every corner. The one on duty in Lake Road (page 30) doesn't look very interested in moving too far from the pub, while his colleague perhaps feels he's more strategically placed outside the National Provincial Bank in Palmerston Road (page 81). And it would be hard to miss the gesticulating, white-coated constable directing traffic at Handley's Corner (page 89).

There are women shoppers dressed in their Sunday best, together with suited men wearing hats. There are children looking like they've just come out of Sunday school, such as those posing for the photographer in Hatfield Road (page 55) and Highland Road (page 70).

It was a different world, perhaps, but fisherman continue 'reelin' in the years' (page 11), soccer supporters never tire of urging Pompey to 'play up' (page 15) and shoppers continue to bustle for bargains (page 66). The queuing tradition endures (page 20) and taxi drivers continue to maintain that things aren't as good as they used to be (page 39).

Many of the evocative images in this book come from postcards – some more than a century old. It is incredible that flimsy bits of card have been passed down and somehow survived through the decades. Postcards remain a rich source of material for local historians and, increasingly, people retracing their family history – from folk collecting images perhaps of churches where their grandparents were married or the warship on which Uncle Jack served.

Postcard collecting was a favourite hobby for many Edwardians at the turn of the last century and the main form of communication between people in the age before the telephone. Although it does not enjoy quite the wide inter-generational appeal today, the hobby is still flourishing, with collectors able to buy from the internet or attend specialist fairs at which some dealers have 'cheap boxes' of the more common postcards for just 20p or 50p each. Some of the postcards that feature in this book are towards the other end of the price scale and one or two of the real photographic examples would cost £30 to £40 each.

In yesteryear, Portsmouth, as a major military garrison and a bustling Royal Navy port, was fortunate in being home to several prolific and highly-skilled photographers of the day such as Stephen Cribb, the Barkshire Brothers, Oscar Owers, Harry Smith and Reginald Silk, men who all helped meet the public's insatiable appetite for new postcards.

It is thanks to their work, and others like them, that we can step back in time and gain this brief glimpse of Portsmouth then and now.

John Sadden and Mark Wingham, 2010

1

LEISURE AND PLEASURE

SOUTHSEA COMMON, *c.* 1907. The importance of freely accessible open space for recreation began to be recognised in the late Victorian period, and it was with great civic pride that Victoria Park was opened in 1878. A Parks and Open Spaces Committee was set up by the Council in 1891 and, as private estates became available, land was acquired for public use, including Alexandra Park (1907), land at Milton (1911, which became Milton and Bransbury Parks), Baffins Park (1912) and the Great Salterns Estate (1926, which became the Municipal Golf Course). Southsea Common was leased from the War Office in 1884 and finally bought by the Council in 1922.

BOATING LAKE IN CHILDREN'S CORNER, SOUTHSEA

CLARENCE PARADE AND Southsea Common, c. 1955. Children's Corner was a popular visitor attraction, and included a paddling pool, swimming pool, boating lake and miniature railway. The Blue Reef Aquarium now occupies this site. The large house, third from the right of the Queen's Hotel, was the Royal Albert Yacht Club but is now the site of a block of flats with an impressive view that is not reciprocated. The growth in car use is evident in the photograph below, which was taken in the early 1990s when the Common began to be used as a car park.

CARRY ON FISHING, *c.* 1908 and 1992. Fishing off South Parade Pier was an activity enjoyed by visitors and locals alike, offering a cheap way to spend one's day with the added thrill of catching the occasional bass or flounder for supper. For some, it was a fun, family activity, while for others it was a refuge from wives and children. According to tourist guidebooks, Southsea's piers offered 'splendid fishing', though South Parade Pier was the most popular, stretching farther out into the Solent and offering an introduction to deeper sea fishing. In the 1920s, Portsmouth had two angling societies, the Piscatorial Society and the Angling Club. The more recent view shows a serious angler on The Hard.

NORTH END SWIMMING Pool, Stamshaw, *c.* 1930. This Council amenity, dating from the turn of the century, was maintained by caretaker Mr George Jones between the wars. He lived in the nearest house on the corner of Strode Road. Bathing costumes could be hired for a halfpenny and many Stamshaw children learnt to swim here. Sadly, it could not compete with the attractions and modern facilities offered by Hilsea Lido, which opened in 1935, and this popular playground in Stamshaw Park now occupies part of the site.

DANCING THE CENTURY away, *c.* 1918 and 2010. While fashions and types of dance change, the love of meeting up and having a good time is a constant, as illustrated here by a romantic, *al fresco*, night-time dance on South Parade Pier, sweetened by a sea breeze, a real orchestra and the gentle background hiss of the surf. The modern view shows a sweaty and thumping night out at the Wedgewood Rooms in Albert Road where, from left to right, Rosie, Ben, Steve, Karen, Dean, Shaun, Diddy, Ollie and Katie push the boat out.

WIMBLEDON PARK PUTTING green and tennis courts, *c.* 1930. Wimbledon Park is the last grassy area remaining of the East Hants Cricket Ground which was bought and built on by developers in the 1880s. On the left is the corner of Lowcay Road and, on the right, the back of houses in Waverley Road. Today, Wimbledon Park serves as a welcome open space and play area for families and a meeting place for young people.

CUPTIE - POMPEY Y BRIGHTON FEB. 15 1913

POMPEY FANS, 1913 and 2009. One spectator at Fratton Park doffs his cap for the photographer at this FA cup tie with Brighton in January (not February as stated on the postcard) 1913, which Pompey lost in front of a gate of 15,556. John Anthony Portsmouth Football Club Westwood has given vocal support at every match, home and away, since 1980. He sports sixty Pompey tattoos and has PFC engraved on his teeth. When he is not supporting Pompey, John runs one of the best antiquarian bookshops in the south of England at Petersfield. The sign above John's right shoulder is believed to refer to an ex-Pompey manager.

LOCKSWAY ROAD, 8 May 1945. Residents are seen here having fun with a pantomime horse and what looks like a carrot and stick at Victory in Europe Day celebrations. In the background is the Old Oyster House which dates from the 1880s, but was rebuilt in 1930 by celebrated local architect Arthur Edward Cogswell. The SWS indicates the presence of a wartime Static Water Supply, a large water tank that was used by firefighters and residents in the event of a loss of supply.

MILTON ROAD

MILTON PARK AND Library, *c. 1925*. The old Milton Public Library, which has been marked with a X on this postcard by the sender, was opened in 1925 in the old Congregationalist Chapel. On the left is the former Middle Farm and, further up, James Goldsmith's Milton Farm which, following his death, was bought by the Council and turned into a park in 1911. This followed public protest at the prospect of it being sold to a developer. On the right is a branch of Smith & Vosper's bakery, a company which started at Kingston Cross in 1806 and flourished until the 1950s, when there were forty branches and 450 employees.

HIGH STREET FROM Battery Row, *c.* 1920. As sightseers view the Square Tower, the horse and cart is parked outside what was the Bell Tavern, which dated from the eighteenth century but was converted to residential use in the 1920s. In the nineteenth century, a Mr Sherwood ran a gunsmith's business from the premises on the far right, and his shooting gallery was used for practise by one of the participants of the last ever duel fought between Englishmen in England, at Browndown, Gosport, in 1845.

ALBERT ROAD, *c.* 1905 and 1991. Visible at the top of this stretch of Albert Road, on the corner of
Exmouth Road, is Ebenezer Perkins' grocery store which was soon to be bought up and demolished,
along with eleven other properties, to make way for the King's Theatre, which opened in 1907.
Built on marshy land, the theatre has a spring under the stage. The building on the right served as
Southsea police station until it was converted into a pub in 1996, the Fuzz and Firkin (the name Pig
and Whistle having apparently not been considered). It was renamed the Goose at the V&A in 2001.

THE HIPPODROME, COMMERCIAL Road, 1911. Queues were an everyday sight on the pavement outside the Hippodrome theatre in this part of Commercial Road, now called Guildhall Walk. Opened in 1907, the venue was marketed as 'the most handsomest and most luxurious house of entertainment on the south coast', and the management guaranteed that performances would be 'at all times refined and of the highest class'. It was bombed in 1941 and the site is now occupied by Hippodrome House and the Walkabout bar, which currently offers a '999 Sexy Services Party' for firefighters, nurses, the police or anyone else who has a uniform. The Nine Elms Tavern, a Victorian pub which stood opposite the Hippodrome, served its last pint of mild in the early 1970s and is now a strip club called Heaven Sent.

EDINBURGH ROAD, *c.* 1910. The Empire Theatre, on the left, is seen here shortly before it was renamed the Coliseum of Varieties in 1913. It reverted to its original name after refurbishment in 1946, but closed in 1959. On the left, at No. 1, is the tobacconist shop run by Adolph Eisner, who was once prosecuted for selling naughty postcards that were alleged to have upset passers-by. His neighbour was Sabatino Pitassi, who ran a sweetshop that was profitably situated next to the Empire. On the far right is the Dental Institute, neighbouring the Albertolli brothers' Swiss Café on the corner of the entrance to the Arcade, opposite Levy the tailor. The rich diversity of nationalities represented by these shopkeepers emphasises that immigration is by no means a modern phenomenon.

THE STRAND, *c.* 1920. This postcard was published by Charles Palmer of No. 101 Clarendon Road, and shows a branch of Timothy Whites drug stores at No. 75. On the opposite corner of Waverley Road is the Granada Hotel, formerly the Granada Arms, which was built in the 1860s. The tiled extension at the front was added in the 1890s but removed during rebuilding in the 1930s. Since the Granada closed in 1985, the building has been used as nightclubs under various names, latterly as the Lounge and Elegance strip club, where customers' anonymity is presumably not compromised by the CCTV camera which has been installed on the traffic roundabout.

THE HARD, *c.* 1910 and 1991. The Victoria & Albert pub dates from around the time of Prince Albert's death in 1861, though it was rebuilt in 1897 by local architect A.E. Cogswell, who was also responsible for the Tudor-style frontage of the Ship Anson in the more recent photograph. The Victoria & Albert was converted to a tobacconist in 1932.

BATH SQUARE, *c.* 1969. The Coal Exchange Tavern dates from at least the 1820s and was described at auction in 1875 as being in an 'exceedingly good position for business on the Point', with 'a spacious bar, parlour, taproom, two kitchens, club room, four large bedrooms and two attics'. In 1991, the Coal Exchange was combined with the Union Tavern and reopened under the name Spice Island Inn (seen here on the right). A pub called the Still dates from the eighteenth century but combined with the West Country House in 1887 to become the Still & West Country House. Popularly known as the Still & West, its rooftop greenhouse, however, proved less popular with the planning authorities.

HIGHLAND ROAD, *c.* 1907. The Royal Marine walking towards the Festing Hotel has just crossed the railway bridge and Albert Road Halt, a station on the short-lived Southsea Railway. The Festing was named after Sir Francis Festing, a Royal Marine Artillery officer and hero of the third Anglo-Ashanti War, who commanded forces against natives defending what was to be later called the Gold Coast. Festing was appointed Colonel Commandant of the Royal Marine Artillery in 1886 but died of natural causes a few weeks later. He was buried in Highland Cemetery, visible at the top of this stretch of Highland Road.

FRATTON ROAD, *c.* 1920. The Home and Colonial tea shop chain operated a branch on the corner of Sheffield Road from the 1890s, opposite the Old Red House public house, which was bombed in 1940 and rebuilt in 1959 as the Unicorn. William Pink set up his first grocery store in Commercial Road in 1858, and by 1939 had forty-seven branches in the area, including this one which closed in the 1970s. The Unicorn was demolished in 2003 and replaced by Pink Court flats.

CASTLE STREET, *c.* 1900. The Wheelbarrow Castle Tavern was renamed the Castle Hotel in the 1860s, and is seen here at the turn of the century when it was run by landlady Miss Alice Collis. In the 1960s it simply became the Wheelbarrow. Comedy actor Peter Sellers visited this area in the 1960s, as his birthplace was a flat above Postcard Corner (now the Mayfair Chinese restaurant), which was an extension of the house on the left, seen here covered in advertisements for local businesses.

HAVANT ROAD, 1900s. Taken from outside a row of cottages called Wellington Terrace, this view shows what looks like a bread and coal delivery to the New Inn. The landlord of this pub during the late Victorian period had the unlikely name of Mr Beerling. Just past the terraced housing in the centre is Drayton Lodge. At the time of writing, the New Inn is being converted into an Indian restaurant.

THE NUFFIELD UNITED Services Officers' Club, 1950s. Opened by Princess Elizabeth in 1951, the Club was intended to offer 'officers and their wives' the opportunity to 'dine, dance and play', the money having been donated by a trust set up by Lord Nuffield. It was sold to Portsmouth Polytechnic in 1978, despite Council opposition that it should be used as a hotel or as a community leisure facility. It now houses the University of Portsmouth Medical Surgery and International Office.

JUNCTION OF LAKE Road and Kingston Road, *c.* 1911. The Tramway Arms stood on the corner of Lake Road, which was realigned to its current position in the 1970s. On the left is Bradbear's tobacconist shop, and on the right of the pub is Buckland Post Office. The Wesleyan Methodist Church, visible in the distance, was built in 1875 and demolished in 1934, its organ moved to Copnor Central Hall, built two years earlier.

2

GETTING ABOUT

HIGHLAND ROAD, EASTNEY, 1962. Trolleybuses superseded trams in 1936 (*see* page 4), and this early colour photograph captures the last days of the trolleybus before motor buses replaced them. Service 17/18 (right) was soon to be converted to motor bus operation, while service 19/20 (left) had switched in 1960.

FESTING ROAD, 1913. The opening of the Festing Road tram route extension is seen here being celebrated by civic dignitaries on the corner of Eastern Parade. This new link connected the Canoe Lake to the public transport network. Fifteen years earlier, Portsmouth Council had voted overwhelmingly to take over the tramway system from private hands because of inefficiency, lack of investment, overcrowded trams and maltreatment of horses. Following the take-over it would also be a great source of revenue for the town.

PORTSMOUTH ROAD, COSHAM, *c.* 1928. This compound served as an off-road turning circle for trams from 1920 and was later the site for an iron shelter for bus passengers which had been relocated from Park Road, but is now in use as a shop in Gunwharf Quays. An eight-storey block of flats, seen here under construction in 2008, now dominates the site. The posters visible on the corner of Windsor Road in 1928 are advertising greyhound racing and two silent movies which were showing at the Regent Cinema in London Road, North End.

DOCKYARD WORKERS, *c.* 1910 and 1939. Dockyard workers leaving work on sturdy bicycles, known locally as the 'charge of the Dockyard light horse', are part of local modern folklore. The photograph below shows their progress past the Coliseum and the Central Hotel on the corner of Edinburgh Road and Commercial Road. At this time, on the eve of the Second World War, there were 15,000 workers employed in the Dockyard.

THE HARD, 1963. At 'outmuster' time, dockyard workers make their way home by car, trolleybus and bicycle. This photograph was taken at the height the Cold War, when employment in the Dockyard was relatively secure. Traffic congestion led to the construction of the 'passenger interchange' in the late 1970s, which extended the carriageway onto a concrete platform built over an acre of the mudflats. The modern view shows a changed skyline, with the power station having been demolished in the early 1980s and the erection of luxury apartments in Gunwharf Quays, previously HMS *Vernon*. The privatised bus service is represented here by a First bus that indicates it is 'Not in Public Use'.

TOWN HALL SQUARE, Commercial Road, 1911. This low-lying area in the centre of town often flooded, even more so when the road surface beneath the upper level platforms of Portsmouth Town Station was lowered to accommodate electric trams. The children are paddling in the area in front of the railway goods shed and yard.

CLARENDON ROAD, 1900s. As one of the lowest-lying areas in Southsea, Clarendon Road was
prone to flooding. This did not prevent a roller-skating rink, designed by local architect G.E. Smith,
being built behind the hoardings, opposite Clarendon Gardens, in around 1914. This site was later
occupied by Wadham Brothers, the motor engineers. Luff's, another motor engineers, traded from
the site on the immediate left for many years. Medford and Tower House flats now dominate the area.

PORTSMOUTH AIRPORT, 1936. The city's municipal airport opened in 1932, boasting an area of over 200 acres with grass landing strips of 2,500ft and 4,500ft, seen here running horizontally, right to left, and diagonally, left to right. The land, much of it having been farmland attached to Highgrove Farm, was drained, cleared and levelled, though the farmhouse was retained as a clubhouse for aviators. The airport closed in 1973, and plans for the area to be largely given over to leisure and recreational use were dismissed in favour of residential development. The Anchorage Park housing estate was built in the 1980s, represented here by its local pub, the Compass Rose.

CABMEN AT FRATTON railway station, *c.* 1930. George Miles (holding the reins of the white horse) and Thomas Elson were the last cabmen in Portsmouth, and are seen on their last day before giving way to the taxi drivers. During the 1920s there were at least twenty-three taxi companies operating in the town. Streamline Taxis was formed in Goldsmith Avenue in 1935, but was taken over by Aqua in 2008. The photograph below shows taxi drivers awaiting fares at Portsmouth Harbour station in 1992.

CAR FOR THE disabled, with Whitbread Brewery in the background, *c.* 1972. Once a major employer, Brickwood's was taken over by Whitbread in 1971 but by 1983 the Portsmouth brewery had closed. Admiralty Quarter was built on the site between 2007 and 2009. Of perhaps more interest in this photograph is the Morris Minor Estate (parked, centre) and the Invacar, a common sight on streets in the 1960s and early 1970s. This light-blue, fibreglass, three-wheeled car for the disabled was affordably leased as part of benefits provided by the National Health Service. Today, mobility scooters, for those who can afford them, compete with pedestrians for pavement space.

3

ON THE STREET WHERE
YOU LIVE

PORTSEA SLUMS, CHATHAM Row and Cross Street, *c.* 1932. These Victorian slums (the wooden house dating from around 1750) appear to have had a high turnover of residents. This included, in the late 1880s, a seven-year-old boy from Chatham Row who was found drowned in the mud in the timber pound on The Hard, the meeting place for the Portsea mudlarks. A house in Chatham Row at this time cost £58, a bargain for unscrupulous slum landlords who could expect to make huge profits exploiting the poor. After the Second World War, Portsmouth Council embarked on an ambitious building programme to provide decent housing, replacing slums that were described as 'a mockery to civilised living'.

ELM GROVE, *c.* 1890. Dr Conan Doyle would have been familiar with this rural view in the heart of Southsea, showing the gateposts of the well-to-do whose grand houses and mansions were set back a safe distance from the road and common people. Conan Doyle, whose practice was on the far left of this view looking west, hoped to attract the sick and rich of Southsea to his modest surgery. The rural nature of the area lasted until 1902, two years after Conan Doyle had left, when most of the old elm trees were cut down to enable shops and business premises to be built on the gardens. The large block on the right of the modern picture, opposite Pelham Road, was built by A.E. Cogswell in 1902-1903.

LANDPORT TERRACE, *c.* 1905. Thomas Mattinson's high-class tailor's was well situated at the junction of King's Road with the genteel residences of Landport Terrace. As an 'agent for Dunhill's Motorites' (the brand name for motoring accessories invented by Alfred Dunhill), Mattinson's might well have stocked the 'Windshield Pipe', which it was hoped would combat some of the difficulties a smoking motorist might face when driving an open-top car. Three doors down, Harold Payne ran his solicitor's practice as well as the local branch of the RSPCA. On the left, a butcher's horse-drawn delivery cart clops along, making deliveries to the Southsea well-to-do.

KING'S TERRACE AND Jubilee Terrace, *c.* 1910. The Terraces were among the first residences constructed in Southsea, built facing the fortifications in the 1810s. In the 1870s, a Mr Henry Collis was operating Turkish baths on the corner of Gold Street and, by the 1910s, it had became the Southsea Turkish Bath & Hydropathic Co. These premises also offered the services of a male and female masseur and, visible on the ground floor, a restaurant. Princes House was later built on this site and occupied by the Inland Revenue.

LONDON ROAD, *c.* 1911. The house on the extreme left, on the corner of Munster Road, was the home of architect Arthur Edward Cogswell, whose family arrived in Portsmouth from Peterborough in the early 1870s. He is most famous for Portsmouth's distinctive half-timbered, turreted and tiled pubs, but also worked on many public and commercial business premises in the town, some of which are featured in this volume. Cogswell died in 1934, though the business was carried on by his sons. The house has continued to have links with property, and has been occupied at various times by Lovegrove's auctioneer, Wilson & Wilson quantity surveyors, Smith & Smith estate agents and Bingley Building Society.

Further up, on the corner of London Avenue, the greenhouses of Burridge's nursery are visible fronting the main road. By the 1930s, Dyer and Huxley's motor engineers had moved in next door and soon the whole corner site was given over to this trade, with Bryant's, Midas Silencers and Boothby's trading here post-war. Kwik-Fit now occupies the site.

GOVERNMENT HOUSE, HIGH Street, *c.* 1878. This large house was the residence of successive naval commanders-in-chief until the 1850s, when the War Office bought it to accommodate the town's garrison commanders. In 1875 the Prince of Wales had luncheon there, apparently without complaint, but a few years later (and notwithstanding the slums that existed a stone's throw away) it was decided that the building was not fit for purpose and a new Government House was built on a site close to the current University of Portsmouth Library.

IRONBRIDGE LANE, MILTON, *c.* 1900. Ironbridge Lane was formerly called Engine House Lane, having been named after the engine pumping house that was built to maintain the water level in the stretch of canal from Milton Road to the sea lock. These five cottages were north of the bridge over the canal, and were sometimes referred to as Milton Cottages. The grounds of Portsmouth Lunatic Asylum (now St James's Hospital) are visible on the left, in what was originally called Lily Lane, then Asylum Road, now Locksway Road.

ST SIMON'S ROAD, *c.* 1905. At the turn of the last century, there were only eight residences in St Simon's Road. Mayville High School for Girls, a part of which may be seen on the left at the end of the road, was originally established in Allens Road in 1897 and is now co-educational.

WHEATSTONE ROAD, *c.* 1905. This street is believed to have been named after the great Victorian scientist and inventor Sir Charles Wheatstone, who died in 1875. Wheatstone invented the concertina and the stereoscope and played a major role in inventing the telegraph. In this residential street, devoid of any sign of telecommunications, local traders G. Cobbett (left), fruiterer, and G. Hatter (right), greengrocer and fruiterer, make deliveries while local children pose for the photographer.

NORTH END AVENUE, *c.* 1908. The only resident in the street in 1888 was an engineer, a Mr Davis, but within a few years the terraces began spreading, built largely by local builder Frank Bevis. The section of road behind the photographer was turned to commercial use to serve the growing population, with Bank Brothers' grocery store on the corner of Gladys Avenue, a bootmaker, hairdresser, newsagent, fish and chip shop, ham and beef shop, greengrocer, dairyman and sweetshop filling the terrace up to Nelson Avenue.

FRATTON, FROM ST Mary's Church tower, *c.* 1920. In the foreground is the Carnegie Library (built by A.E. Cogswell in 1906), while St Jude's spire is visible against the waters of the Solent. In 1929, Fratton Road was widened from Fratton Bridge to St Mary's with many businesses and houses on the east (left) side being demolished. However, the most dramatic change is the loss of much of the terraced housing in Fratton and beyond, to be replaced by blocks of flats of varying size.

LIVINGSTONE ROAD, *c.* 1905. Trade carts add interest to this street scene, and include Hooper's, the fishmongers, on the right. Presumably named after the Victorian explorer, Dr Livingstone, who died in 1873, some of the houses and villas were built with African names, including Nile House, Zanzibar House, Valetort, Rondebosch and Nyanza Villa. The two houses at the far end of the road have been replaced by the Heatherley Court and Chatsworth Court flats.

4

SCHOOL, CHURCH AND COMMUNITY

EMPIRE DAY, 24 MAY 1912. The first Empire Day, organised to celebrate and reinforce the ideals of British imperialism, took place in 1902 on the late Queen Victoria's birthday. A decade later, boys at the old Portsmouth Grammar School were addressed by Major-General Blewitt (right), Commander of the South Coast Defences, who stated that 'our Empire had been won by hard work, pluck and unselfish duty, and if we were to keep our Empire, we must continue to foster those same qualities'. Empire Day was superseded by Commonwealth Day in 1958.

WIMBORNE ROAD SCHOOL, *c.* 1916. Separate schools and entrances for boys and girls were the norm up until the 1970s, visible here at the Evans Road entrances of Wimborne Road Council Schools, taken soon after opening in 1916, two years later than what is set in stone on the left. The school was built by Frank Privett, who was to become mayor twice in the 1920s and '30s. A.E. Cogswell, whose work as an architect is well represented in this volume, was the quantity surveyor. The Victorian belief in the desirability of high windows to prevent pupils being distracted by the outside world appears to have passed.

HATFIELD ROAD, *c.* 1912. Reginald Road School was built in 1906 with a capacity for 390 boys, 390 girls and 440 infants. Parents did not need to worry about road safety, the only traffic visible here being two delivery carts, just past the school on the right. One bears the name of Samuel Knight's bakery in Arundel Street. William Drew's general store, on the corner of Hunter Road, served the neighbourhood with everyday essentials.

Convent of the Cross, Southsea. Front View.

CONVENT OF THE Cross School, Grove Road North, *c.* 1925. This private Catholic girls' school was established in 1902 by a group of Boscombe nuns, though the building itself appears to have been completed in 1907. Order was kept in the early years by a Mother Superior with the surname Grimm. Following its wartime use by the Eye and Ear Hospital, the school re-established itself in Oaklands, Stakes Hill Road, Waterlooville. In 1966, Daley's Grammar School (in Kingston Crescent) amalgamated with Oaklands to become Oaklands Convent School, but is now a co-educational Catholic school and sixth form college. The Eye and Ear Hospital continued operating in this building until 1970, and Homegrove House flats now occupy the site.

SAXE-WEIMAR ROAD, *c.* 1905. Renamed Waverley Road as a result of anti-German feeling during the First World War, the road immortalises Sir Walter Scott's book *Waverley* (published 1914), which is regarded by some as the first historical novel.

St Swithun's Church opened in 1901, replacing an iron church that had been erected in the 1890s, but was relocated to the rear of the current church until its removal in 1983, the same year that the nearby Nazareth House closed. Built on marshy land, by the 1950s the floor of the church had subsided resulting in a situation where, after the knot was tied, grooms were obliged to take their brides up and down and up and down the aisle.

MANNERS ROAD, *c.* 1911. Children make their way down Manners Road, probably to the school in Francis Avenue (both roads were named after local landowners). On the left is James Jones' corner grocery store, and on the right, Albert Knight's booksellers, stationers and tobacconist shop.

VICTORIA ROAD SOUTH, *c.* 1905. The Congregational Church was built in 1883 of iron, and offered a meeting place for separate young men's and women's social clubs and the Band of Hope, a temperance organisation which had its work cut out in Portsmouth. A more permanent structure, which now stands derelict, was erected in 1911 with seating for 550 worshippers.

ST MARK'S CHURCH, Derby Road, *c.* 1935. Built in 1874, St Mark's landmark clock tower was added in 1898 and cost more than the church itself. Up until the 1870s, worshippers had attended services in North End Hall which was situated behind the Clarence Gardens (now called Mischief) pub. In 1923, London Road was widened to accommodate increased traffic and the boundary wall set back. St Mark's was demolished in 1971 and a new church built on the opposite side of Derby Road. The chimney on the left belonged to Northleigh, which became the rectory for St Mark's after the death of its owner John Young, a former mayor, councillor, magistrate and philanthropist.

EDINBURGH ROAD, *c.* 1972. The Congregational Church, seen here during demolition, was built in 1896 on War Office land and succeeded the King Street Chapel which had closed three years earlier. In July 1899, services had to be cancelled due to the serious flooding of the area, filling the church with water 2ft deep. The church was extended in 1930 with seating for 600 worshippers. On the right in Unicorn Road is Whites barber shop and, just visible behind the church, is Ensign Motors second-hand car dealer's forecourt.

MEMORIAL HALL AND St Paul's Church, *c.* 1906. Long's Memorial Hall (left) was built as a school and then became a Baptist chapel, but was in use as business premises at the time this photograph was taken. In 1908 it was given to St Paul's as a church hall by Long, the brewer, in memory of his sons, and is now the site of Southsea Community Centre. St Paul's was built in the early 1820s but was bombed in 1941, the shell and surrounding area later being used by the Royal Marines to practise fighting in an urban environment.

TOWN HALL SQUARE, August 1905. To celebrate the centenary of the glorious victory at Trafalgar (and, incidentally, the Entente Cordiale) a squadron of the French Fleet was welcomed in Portsmouth with a royal review, fête, banquet and garden party. The modern view shows the Bangladeshi flag-raising ceremony held in the Guildhall Square in October 2009, which attracted hundreds of local people who celebrated ethnic diversity in the city.

GONE TO BLAZES, *c.* 1900 and 1991. These firefighters are wearing metal Merryweather helmets and proudly posing on their new, state-of-the-art Merryweather steam fire engine on Clarence Esplanade. Before steam replaced horse-power, the fire brigade's horses were kept in the Corporation Stables in Park Road, next to the Town Hall. The view below shows firefighters of Hampshire Fire Brigade extinguishing a fire at the back of Curtess shoe shop in Commercial Road.

5

SHOPS AND BUSINESSES

COMMERCIAL ROAD, 1972. The town centre remains the city's primary shopping destination, despite the impact of Gunwharf Quays. In this view, taken before pedestrianisation, two public clocks broadly agree on the time of day. Littlewoods, C&A, H. Samuels, Dunn & Co., Burton's, Marks & Spencer's, Meaker's Menswear and Stone-Dri Weatherwear are visible. Under the clock on the right, a boutique selling very Seventies gear traded under the very Seventies name 'Strictly for the Birds'. Next to H. Samuels is the Classic cinema, showing *Blue Water, White Death*, a documentary about white sharks. It shut shortly afterwards, bowing out with a showing of *The Cruel Sea* in August 1972.

COMMERCIAL ROAD, *c.* 1939 and 1978. Congested pavements, with pedestrians spilling onto the busy Commercial Road, were a feature of the city's main shopping area until pedestrianisation in the 1970s. Both these photographs feature Woolworth's store, which was a presence in Commercial Road for over ninety years until its closure in 2009. The site had previously accommodated Barnes & Seager Ltd, wallpaper merchants, Maynard's sweetshop and Hartley's outfitters. C&A's clothes store, seen on the right of the 1978 photograph, closed in 2001.

TIMOTHY WHITES STAFF,
Commercial Road, in around
1922, and Palmerston Road,
1983. Timothy White set up
as a chemist in Portsmouth
in 1848 and qualified as a
pharmacist in 1869. By the
1890s his chain of drugstores
was one of the ten largest in
the country and, at the time of
its takeover by Boots in 1968,
had 600 branches nationwide.
As this photograph shows,
the company had diversified.
By the 1920s, it was offering
'pure drugs, toilet requisites,
photographic materials,
household requisites, brooms,

brushes and mats'. This branch, which was situated opposite the Air Balloon pub in old
Commercial Road, is displaying a selection of both rubber and stoneware hot-water bottles.
The Palmerston Road branch (below) was one of the last survivors of the national chain,
trading as a hardware store before closure in the 1980s.

KINGSTON ROAD, *c.* 1972. Buckland United Reformed Church, which opened in 1869, outlived the Bedford Arms (right) which was demolished in 1974. Both Bray's toyshop (which also sold tobacco and sweets) on the corner of Powerscourt Road, and Brisons' bakery next door, were established in this terrace in the 1960s. Mr Brison retired in 1995 and the shop is now a Polish delicatessen, Slavyanka. Darants butcher's shop is now a tattooist while, further up, Jenours' jewellery shop has diversified into pawnbroking. The rise in the popularity of takeaways is reflected in this short terrace, with Polish, Chinese, Nepalese and Indian cuisine being served from four premises.

KINGSTON ROAD, *c.* 1910. Taken from outside the Wesleyan Methodist Chapel on the corner of Sultan Road, this photograph shows the diversity of small, independent shops that were trading in Kingston Road at the time. The row of eight shops visible on the right extending to New Road included three butchers' shops, two grocers, a fruiterer, a tobacconist and a clothes shop. The shops on the left include a stationer's, a sweetshop, a tea dealer, a wine merchant, a doctor's surgery, a cycle maker, a photography and a sewing-machine shop.

CAMBRIDGE TERRACE, HIGHLAND Road, *c.* 1910. Perhaps Caleb Nancarrow's Dickensian name influenced his choice of pawnbroking as a career (practised from the shop on the left). His neighbour, William William, served the people of Eastney with fish and chip suppers, while Thomas Smith was in business as a corn merchant. Charles Pitt's furniture shop is just visible, far right, and was next door to Eastney Post Office.

HIGHLAND ROAD, *c.* 1906. This row of shops, opposite Eastney Post Office, was briefly named Festing Terrace and included two grocery shops, including Charles Cox's (son of Charles Cox, see page 79), two butchers, a greengrocer, fruiterer, a dairy shop, tobacconist and a sweetshop. By the early 1970s, Butler's cycle, radio and television dealers occupied Cox's premises, and other shops included a hairdresser, a watchmaker, a delicatessen and a record dealer trading under the name Clockwork Banana. The terrace is now entirely in residential use.

SELBOURNE TERRACE, *c.* 1910 and 1991. Fratton Bridge Post Office, run by Joseph Bignell, is on the left, next door to Alfred Payne's bootmaking and repairing business which boasted of using 'English leather only'. Further up, towards Fratton railway station, is Frank Turner's coal-dealing business. The post office later became a branch of the Southsea Dairy Co., then, for over fifty years, a Lloyds Bank (now Band of Gold Bridal House). Agnes Skinner's tobacconist and sweetshop closed in the early 1990s and was converted for residential use.

EASTNEY ROAD, *c.* 1910. Greengrocer Charles Newton's shop at No. 60 Eastney Road was later the premises of John Arkell, the chemist who, after the Second World War, traded from the opposite side of Eastney Road on the corner of Suffolk Road. John Druce's boot shop and cobbler's business, at No. 64, relocated to Highland Road by the 1930s (while another branch run by William Druce opened on the corner of Meon Road and Catisfield Road). The shop next door is advertising itself as an oyster bar, while Watkins' cycle shop hired out bikes and prams by the hour, day or week. The two shops on the left were run by fishmonger Henry Curtis, whose 'Little Billingsgate' is offering fish and rabbits.

COPNOR ROAD, *c.* 1911. Copnor railway bridge opened in 1908, replacing a dangerous level crossing. The prohibitive cost of land meant it was built at a gradient that was far too steep for traffic. Arthur Hooper's grocery store and post office stood on the north side, on the corner of New Road East, next door to Ernest Smith's butcher's shop. The Swan pub, seen in the distance, dates from the 1890s, though a pub called Duncan's Head is believed to have served pints on this site from the 1850s. In keeping with the custom of the time, coroner's inquests were often held in the local pub and those at the Duncan's Head included Copnor's railway signalman who had been accidentally killed on the nearby track in 1869.

ST MARY'S ROAD, *c.* 1907. Pawnbroker's balls are visible (top left) hanging over No. 53, in this view looking east. On the corner of Shakespeare Road is Edward Trevis's grocery shop (advertising Nestlé's milk). This terrace includes Briggs' the drapers; Nathaniel Pilcher, fried fish dealer; Augustus Lockhart, butcher; and William Knight, fishmonger. On the corner of Shearer Road, a stone's throw away from Kingston Cemetery, is Samuel Wells' monumental masonry business.

KING'S ROAD, *c.* 1906. This photograph was taken from outside John Dyer's store, which straddled King's Road with the furnishing department on the left and drapery on the right. Just past Whittington Chambers (on the left) is the turning into Gloucester Terrace, where a protected area of trees remains today. Directly ahead is the Bush Hotel, Bush Villas (where Dr Conan Doyle ran his medical practice from 1882 to 1900) and Elm Grove Baptist Church. King's Road was previously known as Wish Lane because it led to a meadow called Wish situated in the Albert Road area. The bend in King's Road and Elm Grove was straightened and the road widened after wartime bombing.

HIGHLAND ROAD, *c.* 1910 and 1991. John Dyer set up his drapery business in King's Road (opposite Great Southsea Street) in 1862. This branch served East Southsea until it was taken over by David Minter in 1929, who expanded the business, taking in the neighbouring premises in 1946 and seen here trading as Porter Brothers, clothiers. From the 1960s it was known as Bon Marche and continued to be run by the Minter family until closure in 2009.

WINTER ROAD, *c.* 1930. Batchelor & Putman's Bakeries occupied the premises on the corner of Bramshott Road, but by 1960 was one of twenty-seven branches of Smith & Vosper's bakery chain. This terrace of shops was built after the First World War, though the Shepherd's Arms (later renamed the Shepherd's Crook) was built on the corner of Goldsmith Avenue in 1912, replacing a pub of the same name which stood on the corner of Priory Crescent, where the entrance to Milton Park now is.

COX'S GROCERY STORE, Albert Road, *c.* 1905. Charles Cox offered a wide range of dairy products, vegetables and meat from his shop at 124-126 Albert Road. The posters in the window are promoting Cox's Christmas Club, offering an affordable way of buying 'a fine turkey, a prime goose and a 9lb joint of meat'. Cox's son, also called Charles, ran a similar shop in Highland Road (see page 71). Next door is John Harris, a watchmaker, formerly of Clerkenwell, offering 'expert repairs [at this address] since 1897'.

ELM GROVE, 1920s. Included in the shops on the left is that of Louis, which provided the Southsea well-to-do with fashionable furs. The fur-draped ladies on the right have just crossed St Peter's Grove, and are about to pass Gange's, 'the footwear and foot comfort depot', which also had a branch several doors up in the 1930s selling solely Dr Scholl's footwear, as well as a branch in London Road.

CLARENDON ROAD, *c.* 1906. The awnings of Handley's, on the opposite corner of Palmerston Road, are reflected in the windows of the National Provincial Bank on the corner of Clarendon Road. A branch of Porter Brothers' clothes shop is on the right. The clock on the post outside Flora's costumier and milliner's shop suggests the photograph was taken at 10.55 a.m., and the boy who is about to cross the road is clutching a bucket and spade, perhaps returning from Southsea beach. The bank site is now occupied by Knight & Lee's, which moved down from a site north of Stanley Street after the Second World War.

PALMERSTON ROAD, *c.* 1905. A public clock suggests this photograph of an almost deserted Palmerston Road was taken at 7.25 a.m., while the modern view shows Orwellian, round-the-clock surveillance by a CCTV camera, having perhaps replaced the fear of an omnipresent God inspired by St Jude's Church, behind the wall on the right. The buildings visible on the immediate left and St Jude's were the only survivors of wartime bombing in this stretch of Palmerston Road.

PALMERSTON ROAD, *c.* 1909. This photograph was taken from outside Joshua Warsow's cigarette-manufacturing business, one of several that operated in Portsmouth in the early twentieth century to cater for the growing addiction among working people. The shop awning on the right belonged to butcher, William Ford, and on the opposite corner of Stanley Lane is the premises of fishmonger, Robert Gibb, which was soon to be absorbed by Knight & Lee's. On the immediate left is a branch of Timothy Whites drugstores, next door to the Victoria Hotel, and, further up, the Cambridge Hotel.

ALBERT ROAD, *c.* 1905. George Peters' wine and spirit merchant is on the corner of what was still referred to as Beach Farm Road, before being combined with Francis Avenue (named after local landowner, Mr Francis Francis). The Bold Forester pub, which dates from at least the 1870s, is visible at the end of this stretch of road, sporting an advertisement for Long's porter. In Edwardian days, three shops down from Fawcett Road, 'naturalist' Mr Richardson stuffed dead animals for the Southsea gentry.

MILTON MARKET, EASTNEY Road, *c.* 1905. The rows of shops known as Milton Market were built in around 1905 and the grocery shop on the nearest corner of Suffolk Road took on the function of a post office a few years later. The Fort Cumberland Arms (just past Devonshire Avenue) continues to serve pints a century later, having seen off its competitor, the Fort Cumberland Tavern (left), which was rebuilt by architect A.E. Cogswell as the Cumberland Tavern but then eventually turned into flats in 1989. Further up was the site of the Birdcage Club, a meeting place for mods where artists like The Who, Pink Floyd and David Bowie performed in the 1960s. The Eastney Electric Theatre, a 650-seater cinema, was built on the nearest corner of Devonshire Avenue in 1910.

HORNE'S DINING ROOMS, Russell Street, *c.* 1910. With 'all English meat' guaranteed in its hot dinners, John Horne appealed to the patriotism of local people, none more so that during the First World War when he offered soldiers 'home from the front' discounted, wholesome meals. Horne's had another branch in Commercial Road, next door to Mrs Eliza Judd's hotel on the corner of Station Street. John Southey's building business (seen here, left, on the corner of Salem Street) was established in 1893 and rapidly expanded to include warehouses in Sussex Street, showrooms in nearby John Street and a branch in Somers Road. The company was taken over by Holt Ltd in 1919, but continued trading under the Southey name in Portsmouth for many years.

RUSSELL STREET, 1920s. Horne's is on the right of this view of a bustling Russell Street (misspelt on the postcard), which linked Commercial Road (now the Guildhall Square) to Hyde Park Road, and was named after the Russell family, the Dukes of Bedford. John Russell served as Prime Minister twice in the nineteenth century, and his grandson was the great philosopher and ban-the-bomb campaigner, Bertrand Russell. The pub, four up on the left, was called the Duke of Bedford and, next door, was Tanner's umbrella manufacturing establishment. Henry Kimber's wine shop and the Hyde Park Road branch of William Pink's grocery stores are visible at the end of the street.

HIGH STREET, COSHAM, *c.* 1911. Henry Smith's shop, seen on the left on the corner of Havant Road, was one of three butchers' shops in Cosham High Street at this time, the others being run by Frank Burt and Harry Bolt. A popular livestock market was held every Monday, drawing farmers from the local area. Among the businesses further down the High Street were two blacksmiths, two bootmakers, an ironmonger, a corn merchant and a saddler and harness maker.

OSBORNE ROAD, *c.* 1905 and *c.* 1958. The road on the right in the Edwardian view is Portland Road, which was realigned after the Second World War. On the corner is Read & Co., hosiers and tailors, and, just visible next door, Arnold & Son, optician. The post-war view, taken from a point further east, shows the new Handley's store (now Debenhams), rebuilt in 1955 following bombing in 1941, and the Westminster Bank Chambers on the corner of Portland Road.

SULTAN ROAD, *c.* 1972. This rare view of a tripe-dressing factory was taken just before the extensive redevelopment of the Buckland area in the 1970s. Sultan Road is on the left and Prince's Place flats, the only remaining buildings, are visible between the factory and the remaining houses in Prince's Street. Robert Taubman's business operated in Lake Road from the 1910s but relocated to these premises at the bottom of the gardens of these terraced homes. Tripe dressing involved the cleaning and boiling of the stomach lining of cows and infamously smelled strongly of faeces.

KING'S ROAD, *c.* 1905. The only identifiable feature remaining in this view following wartime bombing and redevelopment is the roof of the Clarence Barracks (now the City Museum), visible on the horizon. On the left is a branch of the ubiquitous Timothy Whites' pharmacy, while on the near corner of Hyde Road (right) is rival Thomas Job's chemist shop. Further down, just past South Street on the right, is Joseph Bulpitt's drapery store spanning five shop units. The cyclist (bottom right) is just passing Henry Clatworthy's sweetshop.

GLADYS AVENUE LAUNDRY, *c.* 1972. The Brunswick Laundry was opened in Brunswick Street in 1879 by Mr A.W. White. The business expanded and bigger premises were built in Gladys Avenue (which he was influential enough to have named after his daughter), and a dyeing and cleaning business was added in London Road. Horse-drawn vans were used for collection and delivery, the west side of the laundry building being used for the stables. Mr White also established himself in several other local businesses including the tramway system, furniture removals and storage, Clarence Pier, the Empire Theatre and the telephone system.

A laundry worker in the 1920s perhaps gave some indication as to the secret of Mr White's business success, explaining how, after working ten-hour days from the age of fourteen to sixteen, young workers were given the sack to avoid the payment of the employer's National Insurance stamp. The Brunswick Laundry's biggest competitor was Chapman's, which was established by Elizabeth Chapman as a cottage industry in Hambrook Street in 1887 and rapidly expanded. The Brunswick Laundry was taken over by National Sunlight in the early 1970s.

HIGH STREET, 1868. Taken from outside the old Guildhall and Council Chambers, this view shows its neighbour, the Dolphin Hotel, which dates from the eighteenth century. By the early nineteenth century it had a theatre at its rear, which later became a dance hall and assembly room where smoking concerts took place. On the far corner of Pembroke Road is John (later Henry) Groves' butcher's shop, which became a branch of Smith & Vosper's bakery in 1887 and was rebuilt in the 1950s following wartime bombing of the area.

OLD COMMERCIAL ROAD (Lord Montgomery Way), *c.* 1920. The Water Co. building, seen at the end of this stretch of old Commercial Road, was built in 1883 and is sometimes credited as being local architect A.E. Cogswell's first commission. A landmark building, it was demolished in 1970 to make way for a new road system. The four-storied Charter House, on the right, has dominated this road (renamed Lord Montgomery Way in the early 1970s) since its construction in around 1900. On the left of the recent view is the Café Parisien in the old Commercial Chambers building, a former tax and social security office.

STATION STREET, *c.* 1931.
Mr Madden's restaurant and
hotel business in Unicorn Road
and Station Road was popular
with sailors, providing an
alternative to Aggie Weston's
Royal Sailors' Rest, where the
regime demanded one's soul in
part payment for a bed and meal.
In the 1900s (inset), Mr Madden
boasted of having 'kitchens,
bright and clean as a new pin,
food well-cooked and of the best
quality, and the water supply
beyond reproach', suggesting

that other businesses were less scrupulous. By 1939, the expanded Station Hotel and Restaurant
was offering bed and breakfast for 4*s* 6*d*, though a good night's sleep could not be guaranteed due
to the close proximity of passing steam trains. An easterly breeze would make guests aware of
Portsmouth Fish Market (on the right), now the site of the main post office in Slindon Street.

Other titles published by The History Press

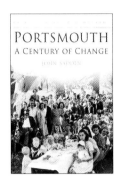

Portsmouth: A Century of Change
JOHN SADDEN

This collection of intriguing photographs cover over a century of Portsmouth's rich history, during which street scenes changed beyond recognition. Communities grew and then were fragmented by war, road schemes and redevelopment. From Victorian spectators at a sports day to punks on Southsea prom, the changing experience of everyday work, leisure and play will delight everyone wanting to discover the Portsmouth of yesteryear.

978 0 7524 4877 0

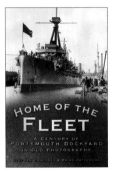

Home of the Fleet: A Century of Portsmouth Dockyard In Old Photographs
STEPHEN COURTNEY & BRIAN PATTERSON

During the past century, the Royal Navy and its support services at Portsmouth dockyard have experienced a pace of change not seen since the fifteenth century. This book examines the impact of that change on the ships, buildings and personnel of the naval base. Richly illustrated with photographs from the Royal Naval Museum and Historic Dockyard collections and exclusive, newly-commissioned photographs, *Home of the Fleet* will appeal to everyone who is interested in Britain's naval heritage.

978 07524 4942 5

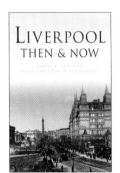

Liverpool Then & Now
DANIEL K. LONGMAN

The popular tourist city of Liverpool has a rich heritage, which is uniquely reflected in this fascinating new compilation. Contrasting a selection of forty-five archive images alongside full-colour modern photographs, this book delves into the dramatic changes to the city. As well as delighting the many tourists who visit Liverpool, this book will provide present occupants with a glimpse of how the city used to be, in addition to awakening nostalgic memories for those who used to live or work here.

978 07509 5740 6

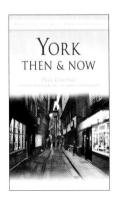

York Then & Now
PAUL CHRYSTAL & MARK SUNDERLAND

The city of York is one of England's most historic and best preserved cities, which is uniquely reflected in this fascinating collection. Contrasting a selection of ninety archive images alongside full-colour modern photographs, each page captures life in the area as it once was – and is now. Featuring streets and buildings, shops and businesses, and the people of York, all aspects of life in the city are covered, providing a fascinating insight into the changing face of the city.

978 07524 5735 2

Visit our website and discover thousands of other History Press books.

www.thehistorypress.co.uk